KEITH HARING

THE BOY WHO
JUST KEPT DRAWING

Kay A. Haring

illustrated by

Robert Neubecker

Dial Books for Young Readers

THERE WAS A BOY NAMED KEITH.

When he was little, his father taught him how to draw dogs and fish and funny things. His dad would draw a line. Then Keith would draw one. Soon, the whole page would be full.

From that time on, Keith never stopped drawing.

In elementary school, while taking tests, Keith doodled on the edge of his paper.

When he handed in his work, his teachers would ask, "WHY did you doodle on this important paper?"

Keith didn't answer.

He went back to his desk and *just kept* drawing.

Sometimes Keith invited his friends to draw in his backyard clubhouse.

Keith made symbols and said
each one represented a letter of the alphabet.
His friends asked, "WHY do you use symbols to write?"

Keith drew more symbols.
It was his way of answering their question.
He encouraged his friends to join him.

As a teenager, Keith liked to draw in his bedroom with music playing LOUD. He would draw on every piece of paper he could find.

His mother had to yell over the music, "WHY can't you turn that music down and go outside to ride your bike?"

But Keith had sold his bike to buy art supplies, so he answered, "Look at the cool drawings I did." And he just kept drawing.

When Keith was in high school he won FIRST PRIZE for his art. A successful couple from town offered to buy his drawing. Keith said, "No, thank you. If you enjoy my art, you may hang it on your wall—no charge!"

Keith's sisters were shocked. "WHY didn't you take the money?" they asked.
Keith shrugged. He just wanted to keep drawing.

Keith graduated from high school and went to the big city of Pittsburgh to a school that would teach him about art. There were boys on the street trying something new—break dancing. He liked the crazy shapes of their bodies as they turned and flipped on the ground. While the music played loud, Keith started drawing wiggly lines.

His teachers asked him, "WHY are you drawing pictures that look like scrambled bodies? This is not what we told you to draw."

Keith knew how to draw. He just wanted to draw in different ways.

And he kept drawing.

Keith moved to the HUGE city of New York when he was twenty, so he could draw with other artists. He started to draw all over the city—on walls, on sidewalks, and on paper that he hung on lampposts. His drawings were washed away by the rain or torn down by street cleaners.

Other artists asked Keith, "WHY do you draw in places where your pictures are erased?"

Keith didn't hear them.
He was searching for another wall so he could keep drawing.

Keith got a job delivering packages and sometimes rode the subway. One day, he saw a panel of black paper on the wall in a station. He rushed outside to buy chalk and came back and began to draw. The white chalk made bright, smooth lines on the black paper. Day after day, Keith filled the empty panels in the subway stations with art.

Soon people who rode the subway were looking for the white chalk drawings. No one knew the name of the artist, but his drawings were easy to recognize.

People asked him, "WHY are you drawing here? What do your pictures mean?"

Keith said, "What do you see? You decide what they mean."

Where Keith lived there was trash on the street and people didn't always say hello to each other. One day, he and his friends cleaned up twenty bags of garbage in front of a long wall. Then Keith painted square faces with smiles and body shapes dancing upside down. The neighbors liked the drawings and stopped to say thank-you.

DISCOUNT SHOES

A policeman came by and lectured Keith.
"WHY did you do this? I have to give you a ticket because you didn't get permission."
Keith paid the fine and just kept drawing.

Soon people wanted to see more of Keith's drawings, and he was asked to display his work in an art gallery. Art was hung from floor to ceiling, and in between he painted on the walls. Keith invited everyone to come and enjoy his work.

All of Keith's artwork SOLD. The gallery owner asked him, "What are you going to do with all this money?"

Keith said, "I read in the newspaper that there are kids who don't have enough to eat. I didn't have this money yesterday and I was happy. If I don't have it tomorrow, I'll still be happy. All children need to eat. I'll send the money to them."

The gallery owner gasped, "WHY?"

Keith just smiled and started to draw again.

Now people were inviting Keith to draw in famous museums and exhibit in galleries all over the world. He was proud that he had become a successful artist. But wherever he went, Keith insisted he paint a mural so EVERYONE could enjoy his work— not just the people who had money to buy it.

During a visit to Paris, France, Keith painted on the outside of a children's hospital—six stories high.

Newspaper reporters came to take pictures and asked, "WHY did you paint at the hospital? Do you think it will make the sick children feel better?"

Keith didn't have time to answer. He had to finish the painting.

When the Statue of Liberty was 100 years old, Keith drew
an outline of the famous statue on a huge piece of vinyl fabric.
Then he asked 900 kids to help him finish the drawing.

Keith told them, "Draw anything. Whatever you want.
No one can say it's bad or good. It's yours."

When the giant painting was displayed, people were amazed to see what Keith and the kids had made.

But the art critics couldn't understand WHY a famous artist was drawing with kids.

But you know Keith . . . He just kept drawing.

Keith painted all over the world.

He would draw on anything, anytime, anywhere.

Wherever he went and whatever he did—he would not stop.

He just kept drawing.

Now everyone wanted to know . . . and together they shouted . . .

"WHY????"

"WHY do you draw all the time?
WHY do you give your artwork away?
WHY do you draw on buildings, on people, on clothing, on furniture, on subway walls, on cars, on skateboards, on walls that belong to no one, and on things to be thrown away?
WHY do you draw on EVERYTHING??"

Keith stopped drawing, just for a moment, and answered:
"I draw all the time because there are many spaces to fill. I give my drawings away to help make the world a better place. I draw everywhere because EVERYONE needs art!!"

Then Keith turned back to the street, took a piece of chalk from his pocket . . .

and just kept drawing.

AUTHOR'S NOTE

I wrote this story to answer the question I'm always asked, "What was Keith like as a kid?" The answer is, "HE WAS ALWAYS DRAWING!"

When we were growing up, our dad was a great inspiration. We'd substitute time in front of the TV with drawing at the kitchen table. During church services or school concerts, Dad would doodle in the margin of the program, and pass it on for us to add our own drawings. Mom would proudly display our artwork on the refrigerator.

Keith's lifelong love of creating art developed into an extraordinary commitment to making art accessible to all people. And he worked hard. Even after achieving great fame, he would often return to New York City from an exhibit overseas and get to the subway as soon

Keith, age 12

as possible to draw there, saying, "The people riding the subway need art, too."

Keith believed, "There is good in everyone and I concentrate on that." He lived his life according to this principle and treated everyone, from young children to famous celebrities to world leaders, in the same respectful, friendly manner.

Keith's exhibition openings were a testament to this. In attendance was a fascinating array of celebrities, families with young children, graffiti artists, people who had never set foot inside a gallery before, and wealthy art collectors. It was always a diverse crowd, all brought together by his dynamic personality and vibrant artwork.

What I most want people to remember about Keith is his deep commitment to community and his unending generosity. There was something magical about how the more he gave away,

Keith, age 14

more doors were open to him, and he used that as a springboard to reach even more people.

Keith's energy and ideals live on in his works of art all over the world and in the ripples of inspiration he started that have echoed around the globe. His enduring legacy is captured best in his most well-known icon. Keith's "crawling baby"—known better as the Radiant Baby—radiates his love for children, celebration of life, and passion to spread art around the world.

Kay, age 2, and Keith, age 4

Haring siblings (from left to right), Kristen Alynne, Karen Aileen (top), Kay Adele (bottom), Keith Allen, age 17.

County, Pennsylvania, our family home. The Youth Advisory Committee (YAC) of Berks County Community Foundation empowers high school students to address issues facing young people in their community by raising and distributing funds to meet those needs. Find out more at www.bccf.org.

 *Kay*

To honor my brother's spirit and pay tribute to a life devoted to celebrating the goodness in all human life, a portion of my proceeds from the sale of this book will be donated to an organization that benefits the youth of Berks

Haring family, Christmas 1971

ABOUT KEITH HARING

Keith Haring is one of America's best-known and loved artists of our age. He was born May 4, 1958, and grew up in the small town of Kutztown, Pennsylvania. He was the eldest of Allen and Joan Haring's four children. His younger sisters were Kay, Karen, and Kristen, and the family dog was named Mumbo. He learned basic cartooning from his father and was inspired by the popular culture of the time, such as Dr. Seuss and Walt Disney. He was always interested in art.

After graduating from high school in 1976, Haring enrolled in the Ivy School of Professional Art in Pittsburgh. He soon realized he had little interest in becoming a commercial graphic artist and moved to New York City in 1978, to attend the School of Visual Arts, where he found a thriving alternative arts community developing on the streets, outside the traditional gallery and museum system.

Haring started drawing in New York's subways in 1980 and by 1985 had produced hundreds of these rapid, recurring line drawings, creating as many as forty in a single day. By expressing universal concepts of birth, death, love, and war—using just a simple chalk line—he created a universally recognizable visual language. Beyond the subway, Haring was experimenting with various mediums, like acrylic paints and Sumi ink, and began using larger surfaces—found objects and canvases. He quickly saw that his audience was expanding from the streets to galleries and museums; sometimes he collaborated with children on public projects, and he often painted in the presence of people so he could engage an immediate response.

Haring's work became popular all over the world. He produced whimsical, colorful art that was understood and appreciated by everyone. There was joy and freedom expressed in his work, and it attracted fans of all ages because of its relevant subject manner and straightforward line. His approach was to start to draw at one end of a space and work across it, with no preplanned sketch, the lines flowing from his hand onto the canvas in a continuous free-form creation.

By 1986, he was commanding huge sums of money for his art. He was determined, however, to devote his career to making artwork available to as wide an audience as possible. In April of that year, Haring opened the Pop Shop, near his studio in Soho, to sell T-shirts, toys, posters, pins, magnets, and many other items bearing reproductions of his images. The Pop Shop was a place where anyone could afford to buy one of his famous images.

He also devoted much of his time to producing art that contained messages about how he felt people should be treated—with respect and equality. He produced more than fifty public works in dozens of cities around the world, most of which were created for charities, hospitals, and children.

During his brief but intense career, Haring's work was featured in over one hundred solo and group exhibitions. In 1986 alone, he was the subject of more than forty newspaper and magazine articles. He was highly sought after to participate in collaborative projects and worked with artists and performers as diverse as Madonna, Grace Jones, Bill T. Jones, William Burroughs, Timothy Leary, Jenny Holzer, Yoko Ono, and Andy Warhol.

In 1989, Haring, who was gay, established the Keith Haring Foundation, to provide funding to AIDS organizations and underserved youth, and to expand the audience for his work through publications, exhibitions, and licensing of his images.

Keith Haring died of AIDS-related complications at the age of thirty-one on February 16, 1990. He used his imagery during the last years of his life to generate activism and awareness about AIDS. And he feverishly traveled the world and continued drawing up until the last few weeks before his death.

The work of Keith Haring is still immediately recognizable and can be seen today in exhibitions and collections of major museums, and in millions of homes around the world.

Keith, age 27, in his New York City studio

KEITH HARING ART APPEARING IN THIS BOOK

Keith Haring artwork © Keith Haring Foundation

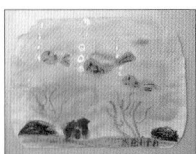

Untitled, 1965
8" x 10", Crayon and
watercolor on paper

A second-grade
school project

Untitled, 1962
4" x 5", Pencil on
paper

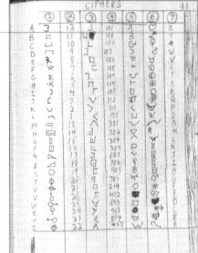

Untitled, 1971
8" x 11", Pen on paper

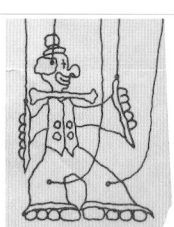

Untitled, 1973
2" x 8", Pen on paper

Untitled, 1977
8½" x 14", Pen and watercolor on paper

Keith drew this for his youngest sister
Kristen for her 7th birthday.

Untitled, 1971 or 1972
6" x 18", Pen on paper

**Three of the Most
Beautiful Pigs in
Pennsylvania,** 1975
5" x 8", Ink and
watercolor on paper

**Finding a Design in
a Face,** 1976
8" x 11", Ink on paper

Sitting Behind Bach,
July 1977
11" x 17", Ink on paper

Untitled, 1975
9" x 12", Ink on paper

Untitled, 1976
30" x 36", Ink and watercolor on paper

Island Lady, 1977
11" x 14", Ink on paper

Untitled, 1981

Untitled, 1981

Untitled, 1981

Untitled, 1982
Fluorescent Day-glo enamel paint

In 1982, Keith Haring created his first significant
outdoor mural on a wall at Houston Street and
Bowery in New York City. The mural has since
been painted over.

Untitled, 1983
Chalk on paper

Keith admired graffiti art, and in
the 1980s he began making chalk
drawings in the subway, sometimes as many as 40 a day, work-
ing quickly as people gathered to
watch. They were quite simple
with figures of barking dogs,
crawling babies, and pyramids, but
instantly recognizable.

Untitled, 1984
80" x 42", Chalk on paper

Untitled, 1982
72" x 72", Acrylic on vinyl tarpaulin

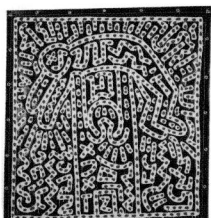

Untitled, 1982
72" x 72", Acrylic on vinyl tarpaulin

Untitled, 1982
72" x 72", Acrylic on vinyl tarpaulin

Untitled, 1982
72" x 72", Acrylic on vinyl tarpaulin

Untitled, 1982
72" x 72", Acrylic on vinyl tarpaulin

Untitled, 1987
31" x 43", Sumi ink on paper

(Below) **Untitled**, 1982
Detail
Acrylic paint on wall

This line of figures, painted right on the wall, brought life to the Tony Shafrazi Gallery, where Keith's work was exhibited.

Untitled, 1987
6 stories, Mural

Over the course of two days, Keith Haring used a cherry picker to paint a mural on the exterior of the Necker Children's Hospital in Paris, France. Many of Keith's philanthropic endeavors brought art to children's hospitals and schools.

CityKids Speak on Liberty, 1986
Detail
90 feet tall, Paint on fabric

Keith Haring, along with the CityKids Foundation, created the enormous work known as the Liberty Banner. It was created over a three-day period at the Jacob Javits Center. The Statue of Liberty was one of Keith's most beloved images.

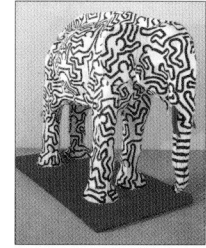

Untitled, 1985
63.87" x 38.12" x 85.75", Acrylic on papier-mâché

Untitled, 1988
Enamel on carbon disk wheels

(Left) **Untitled**, 1982
14" x 17", Felt-tip marker on paper

Additional Art Contributions in This Book

Crown

Jean-Michel Basquiat

© The Estate of Jean-Michel Basquiat

The three-pointed crown was a symbol of Jean-Michel Basquiat, who also did street writing and art in the 1980s.

Graffiti tag

Kenny Scharf

© Kenny Scharf

Kenny Scharf is an artist who was a close friend of Keith Haring and worked alongside him in the 1980s.

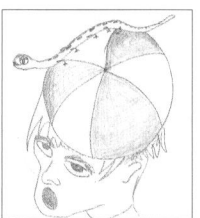  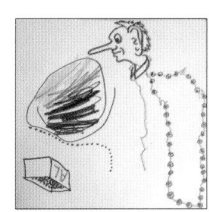   

Untitled drawings by Allen Haring. Allen Haring, Keith's father, did artwork with Keith, Kay, and their siblings and continues to draw with his grandchildren and great-grandchildren.

For all the Harings,
who just keep drawing
—K.H.

For Isidore
—R.N.

ACKNOWLEDGMENTS

For their endless support and faith I thank; Lucia Monfried, editor extraordinaire; Jasmin Rubero, Nancy Conescu, The Keith Haring Foundation, Kenny Scharf, David Stark and the Basquiat family, Mom & Dad, Karen, Kristen, Thea, Maryanne, Lana and Yenna, and my partner in all things, Tom Wessner.

Permission for the use of art by Keith Haring has been granted by the Keith Haring Foundation. Details at the end of the book.
Keith Haring artwork © Keith Haring Foundation

Dial Books for Young Readers
Penguin Young Readers Group
An imprint of Penguin Random House LLC
375 Hudson Street, New York, NY 10014

Library of Congress Cataloging-in-Publication Data
Names: Haring, Kay, author. | Neubecker, Robert, illustrator.
Title: Keith Haring : the boy who just kept drawing / Kay Haring ; Illustrated by Robert Neubecker.
Description: New York : Dial Books for Young Readers, 2017.
Identifiers: LCCN 2015049501 | ISBN 9780525428190 (hardcover) | Subjects: LCSH: Haring, Keith—Juvenile literature. | Artists—United States—Biography—Juvenile literature. | Drawing—Juvenile literature. | Classification: LCC N6537.H348 H37 2017
DDC 741.092—dc23 LC record available at http://lccn.loc.gov/2015049501

Printed in China

3 5 7 9 10 8 6 4

Design by Jasmin Rubero
Text set in Graham Regular with AuoxPro OT

The illustrations for this book were created with a Mac computer and a #2 pencil from personal photos and fond memories of the downtown art scene of the 1980s.